Evolution of the Soul

Alexandria Rossillo

BookLeaf Publishing

India | USA | UK

Presentation by *BookLeaf Publishing*

Web: www.bookleafpub.com

E-mail: info@bookleafpub.com

ISBN: 9789360948993

First edition 2024

Ghazal of an Almost Duck

It was the last day in Canada, the sun
A fading 100-watt light bulb when I saw the
loon.

A shadow on darkened water, it floated by
Same as my line, in a diamond pattern with
others, the loon.

Light sprinkled on water, gathering everything in
Its path, including the loon.

I watched, entranced as it gave its odd squawk,
Spooked and disappeared like a mirage
underneath the waters, the loon.

Deepest Dark

Whispers wind in deepest dark
Evening passes most unseen
Soft light calls from midnight's lark.

Spring ignites from winter stark
Rebirth for a single green
Whispers wind in deepest dark.

Petals wait for daylight's hark
Only then can red be seen
Soft light calls from midnight's lark.

Sunlight spills and finds its mark
Bright red fills the worldly scene
Whispers wind in deepest dark.

Spring has sprung in lush Green Park
Showing gardens rose like sheen
Whispers wind in deepest dark
Soft light calls from midnight's lark.

Black Death

Inching along step by step
Closer to the prize than she's ever been,
The black environment around her
Whispers water as she runs fingers
Along the hood of the car beside her.
The gate hangs open on its hinges
Inviting her into dark depths,
And she pads lightly, hopping
Across hexagonal stepping stones.
The basement door swings open,
Guiding her into his realm,
The underground cave,
His lair.
He's there; sitting, waiting, inviting,
Watching as she sits next to him,
Envelopes herself in his embrace,
And dies happy.

All Better

I was only 14
When I walked through the double doors.
My aunt had collapsed again,
We were going to see her.

As I looked at her,
I saw the starkness of her skin,
The dullness in her eyes like a slap in the face.
She was a skeleton with a skin-like covering.

Tubes in her nose just didn't look right.
I could feel my courage failing.
Like a vampire's victim,
It was drained from my body.

Turning to the heart monitor,
It beeped…beeped…beeped,
The skinny peaks at each second
Marched across the screen in a horizontal
pattern,
Like an army of angry green soldiers.

The stick branches of a tree outside
Scratched against the window pane.
She beckoned me over,

Shifting the IV tube in her arm,
Placing a small tacky looking box in my hand.

There was nothing in it,
It was empty, devoid of anything but colored
strips
Of paper.

     "It's a dream box," she said, "I made it.
Put your dreams in it,
     And they will come true."

I cradled that box to my chest when I was told
she passed on…
Peacock feather on top, glitter, and all.

Blue Moon Cafe Rock

Bartender sashays back to the bar
Across a checkered floor of black and white.
Hotel California serenades her stride
The bar escorting her like a waltz down the
aisle;
She's patience and grace, mixing drinks,
Sliding beer into patrons' hands at a dizzy pace.
She's wild and carefree,
guiding her herd with a timeless elegance.

Eulogy of a Great Woman

Deep-set green eyes twinkle with knowledge
Beneath a pure white halo
Staring at the crowd below her.

Touch an arm here;
Squeeze a shoulder there;
Wipe a tear from the eye of a brother.

"Don't be sad;
Smile for me-I'm safe, warm, and happy!
I'm here with you in your heart!

I've seen so, so much;
-Horse and Buggy, Flappers, Women's Rights-
-Depression, War, Birth of the Modern Age-

I'm always here, always with you;
Just a whisper away.

The voice on the wind;
A kiss of sunlight on your cheek;
The soft touch on the flesh of your arms.

I'm here; always with you."
The angel moved among the crowd,

A beacon of warmth for the remaining family
members.

"I love you all."
A bell rung in the distance.
A bright light shining from above.

She turned deep-set green twinkling eyes up,
Gazing at the heavens,
Unfurling purest white wings.

Taking one last look at the tears of those around
her,
A powerful thrust sends her high to the sky;
A new guardian angel is born.

Staccato

9

Broken bits and pieces fly
like ashes scattered on the wind, a bonfire
burning staccato holes in the membranes of my
soul,
warmth for a second;
blasted cold for a lifetime.

Sweet kisses I have few
taken from broken bits and pieces
a history of warm embraces,
like sweet ambrosia,
waiting for the cold to fall away.

Roaming

Silenced words upon the hill,
Half-baked promises assigned to thrill,
Another girl goes down for the kill;
She's waiting for your hand.

A comment lost to wrinkled hearts,
A biker's thrill rides on the starts,
A lost connection gains the darts;
She's falling into dark.

The final chime falls in darkened grounds,
A yearlong hunt from hell's own hounds,
The body falls in zero sounds;
You've lost her to the shades.

Masquerade

Gown of purest gold,
Silver stitching
Fluffed in back
The new style of dress wear.

The finest ivory corset,
In all the French quarter,
Able to make a women so small,
A man could put his hand
Entirely around her waist.

Blond hair tied back,
Strung with pearls,
Emeralds clasped through light curls.

Dainty mask,
Held close at hand,
The angel walks in,
Suitors already asking
For the first dance.

Mask on face,
She walks past them
To her fiancée,
Kisses him on the cheek,
And watches as the festivities
Take place.

One Lane Road

Deep in the woods, high in the mountains
Over the River, and through the clouds
Next to the bridge where you'd swam
underneath
In the twilight of an everlasting summer.

Follow the taillights of the beckoning vehicles
The flashing lights signaling your end and a new
beginning.
Keeping pace with the vultures above
As life in the slow lane passes you by.

Peace

13

Sun seeps lightly
Through darkened blinds.
Sleeping softly, fiery angel,
Her hair a halo around her head.
Breathing a dove's sigh,
Her face displays serenity
As eyelashes flutter upwards.
Blinking blue eyes glitter in morning light.
"Good morning, Angel. Welcome to sunshine."

Laughter

Laughter like luscious chocolate
Rings through the house.
She's waiting for the clock to stop,
Time to freeze,
When she can have her hay day
Once again.
When life can be happy once more,
In the arms of a goddess.

She Rises

15

First thoughts as she rolls out of bed
Are of brightness, neon yellow.
Slowly, she begins to rise,
Knowing she's needed,
She's a mother to her children.
Hair standing on end,
In pinks, blues, yellows, reds, oranges,
Fingers grasping the mountain tops,
Pulling upwards.
Peeking her eye over the top of the valley,
She sets the houses up in flames
Their windows a bonfire.
Standing up straight
Her head in the clouds,
She moves up and out,
A beacon of warmth for the rising day.

Imagination

Leaning on my window ledge, I sat and watched
the sky,
An endless clashing of star bright blue
against blushing pinks and an orange halo,
Streams of cotton clouds misting the open air,
Failing sunlight covers me through the panes of
old-fashioned windows.

As I sat, I watched the world darken.
The clouds, rolling and tumbling, shadows in the
night.
The sky, a brilliant backdrop of deep blue
Overriding the sunset shades, pushing them
away,
Winds commanding, churning against the
horizon.

There is no sound except that of my family
Stirring in the house below.
Outside, arcs of light finger across the dark
expanse,
brightening my features,
And in that single flash, my eyes narrow—
something in the distance.

A being—a figure—winging gracefully in the
shadows of lightning,
Flying gracefully towards my cottage.
Fingers tighten on my mug as it lands on my
front yard, it's wings...
Pitch black and nearly twice its body length
tucking onto its long form,
Hair tied back, reflecting the blue-black rolling
above.

An outfit, billowing backward in the sharp
winds,
rain plastering the folds of the gown to a figure,
tall—taller than normal.
As it turns its gaze upwards,
my breath catches—the eyes! —Golden—
gleaming in the dark outside, reflecting—
shining.

Barely even registering how I know—She! —
walks towards the cottage, floating through the
sideways rain,
her wings shifting as she steps through the front
door, I sit, listening.
Not even a gasp of wind from outside in the
silence.
Faintly, I hear a dull thud on the floor
downstairs.

I barely register three more thuds following the
first,
Nor do I seem to care that I am the last person
awake in the cottage,
I only barely stir as my door swings open on
silent hinges,
Turning to see the figure from below,
come to collect.

She stood in the doorway, hair misted, but dry,
A dress of black lace under a cloak of starshine,
Pale skin peeking over the bodice, the bottom
dragging.
She tilted her head at me; I understood my fate.
Placing my tea on the windowsill, she knew I
accepted her gift.

Striding forward on silent steps, she raised her
hand,
She held no warmth as her hands cradled my
face— gentle.
Not a word was said.
No goodbyes. No prayers.
Just peace.

I drifted, falling—sighing into an Eternal Sleep,
The knowledge that when I opened my eyes
again, I would be new,

whispering sweet promises to me out of the
darkness.
I felt nothing, tranquility soothing my limbs.
I needed this, an inner peace.

Pulling out of my dream through the window of
my eyes, I smiled.
Above me, a fire in the heavens of reds and
oranges,
fighting back the blues and blacks of nighttime
Overriding; The Heavens turned violet,
and I alone knew the truth.

I met the Angel of Death with peace,
With Grace, I had survived;
My body had moved on to the Heavens.
I hadn't a single care in the world that could
falter
my imagination.

Ying and Yang

Shadows danced around corners
playing hide and seek with the sun;
captured daylight blinds brown eyes
when the moon begins its lullaby.

Sleepy sun lifts her head high
searching for whispers in darkened rooms;
distant moonlight stings grey eyes
when the burning sun reflects starlight's kiss.

She Danced in Moonlight

21

She Danced,
Wind blowing her grey shirt tight
Around the taut flesh of her stomach,
Dark brown hair haloed against the streetlight.

She Danced,
Eyes closed and face raised to the moonlit skies
Drowned in the lunar rays of night,
Her arms bent seductively, curved around her
head.

She Danced,
Brown eyes searching for new suitors,
Hips gyrating against music blasting from her
car,
Howling, lifting her head to the heavens.

She Danced,
Revealing broad expanses of muscle
And slender neck.
In the moonlight, she danced.

Valentine

She held in her hand a card,
A red heart, shaped similarly.
Inside, a cheesy poem:
> 'Roses are Red,
> Violets are Blue,
> Sugar is sweet,
> But I love you.'

Around it, hundreds of hearts
Drawn in black ink—inerasable.
Big, small, perfect, misshapen.
Hearts within hearts within hearts.
She placed both hands
On top of the paper card.
The sound shredding the air
Equaled her sobs as she raised her hands,
Releasing thousands of red tears to the wind;
A parade of solemn red butterflies drifting to the
distance.

Number 2

Guns blazing; scythe gone swinging,
God of Death he comes in singing.
Songs of death and morbid woe
Punched tickets he'll surely sow.

You've seen his face; he cannot lie
Scream your prayers and say goodbye.
A final blow; fires run raging
To hell for Special Oz Scum: caging.

Number 3

A jester's mask adorns his face,
While knives soar through his personal space.

The crowd goes wild, spotlight shining,
Gunner uncovered; blown the lining.

A sister's tears sear deep inside,
'There's more to life than death,' she cried.

The lions roar signal end of show,
Back to the darkness jester's smile goes.

Number 4

25

Musical assassin, apologies given;
Not the pacifist life he's living.

Gentle soul; switchblade mindset
Blow the colony to get his life back.

Love comes calling; lost in space
Ten thousand years can never replace.

Amnesiac blown; Hero Zero come calling;
Tactical genius as Libra is falling.

Evolution of a Girl I am From

I am from grid-iron streets,
Adjacent to a city that never sleeps,
Where life in "The Jungles" was dog-eat-dog,
And Irish Italian was a must not a possibility.

I am from trees standing double taller than
houses,
Animals at five-hundred feet in broad daylight
dumpsters,
Country roads cruising at fifty past onions fields,
Where streams and rivers converge in reservoirs
not sewage.

I am from ocean spray and shoebies
Where the surf heals all wounds;
Children's eyes twinkle against toy-filled glass
cabinets,
But love abounds over endless sunshine.

I am from a return to endless trees and country
roads,
Drive-in movies under black skies and white
fuzzy dots,

Late night runs to midnight escapades lead to
lately early activities,
And life as it is, is from itself to myself.

9 789360 948993